ב"ה

Dear Do
You
lucky yo
natural
Have a wonderful ... y
with Bex!
With my love,
Gillian
x

The Expert's Guide To Speaking in Public

Revealing the best-kept Secrets of Top-Notch Speakers

By

Gillian Cohen FLCM

Published by
The Maven Publishing Co. Ltd
www.mavenpublishingcompany.com

First published in 2007

by
Maven Publications
193a Ashley Road,
Hale
Altrincham
Cheshire
WA15 9SQ

Designed and typeset by MordTzvi Design.
Printed and bound in Great Britain.

This book is dedicated to my wonderful family

About the Author

Voice Coach, Gillian Cohen FLCM has taught, examined and lectured in Voice, Speech & Drama and Presentation Skills for over 20 years.

She has a wide experience teaching in the public and private sector, in education and in commence. Her work takes her from Acting and Voiceovers, to Presentations, Staff Training and Business & Management Courses.

By the same Author:

Our Living Language

ISBN 0-9528375-2-8

Published by LCM Publications

Contents

Foreword

Speaking in public can be seen as an ordeal that many of us shy away from. How many of you reading this, acknowledge that you're almost tempted to risk losing that promotion, rather than have to get up on your feet and speak in front of a group of people on a regular basis?
And if you're worried about that important meeting or interview, you'll know how vital it is to create the right impression.

Speaking in public these days is no longer reserved for special occasions. Once again it's becoming part of our everyday lives, but a skill that's been neglected due to modern technology.
I think that we all agree that to be able to communicate with ease is one of the greatest assets any of us can possess.

And, if you're the Father of the Bride, The Groom or The Best Man – though it may not be an everyday occurrence, why spoil the happy occasion by worrying about the task ahead?

Speaking in public means that once you're up on your feet, you're on show, the centre of attraction.
Why not learn to make the best of it and enjoy every moment?
You can and you will, I promise!

Introduction

I've developed and taught my 7 Step Programme over the past few years, in response to those of you who have come to me in a state of panic, needing help quickly! So many of you put a great deal of time and effort writing out your talks or presentations but give little thought to the delivery of those words until the last minute. Therefore, I've had to devise a programme that is simple but effective and works every time.

As we go through the 7 Steps you'll discover the habits and strategies that Top-Notch Speakers use. Speaking in Public will no longer be a major source of concern for you, dismissed as an accomplishment for the gifted few.

Some of you have confessed how embarrassed you feel, as an adult, to be acquiring skills you feel you should have learnt long ago. Interestingly more people come to me for one-to-one tuition rather than group lessons and so it is with this in mind that I've written this book, which you can read in the privacy of your own home or office.

As a Voice Coach, with over 20 years experience, I specialise in Voice, Speech and Presentation Skills. I know that it is not so much what you say but ***how*** you say it, that in the end, guarantees a winning performance.

I do admit there's a great deal of mystique surrounding the subject of Public Speaking. Everyone I've ever taught has been pleasantly surprised that the skills learnt haven't been as difficult or time consuming as they'd once imagined. Obviously if you've a speech, presentation or interview looming ahead you're going to be more motivated to ***apply*** the skills you've learnt and also so relieved to find out it isn't all quite so terrifying as you once thought.

I'm going to show you that my 7 Step Programme will enable you to get up on your feet and enjoy being yourself (albeit a slightly larger-than-life version). Lesson No. 1 is always – don't try and adopt a 'Public Speaking Persona'. Every one of you is unique and we want your personality to shine through. You too can become a memorable speaker and make it an rewarding experience!

Let's find out the devices Top-Notch Speakers use to look so much in control. I hope you find these 'Trade Secrets' useful too!

1 Preparing Yourself

1 Preparing yourself

You've been asked to 'say a few words' or to introduce a speaker or give a vote of thanks. Maybe you're the 'Keynote' speaker to raise funds or woo voters. You want to influence or persuade the audience. Perhaps you're the Groom or the Father of the Bride or the Best Man or, maybe you're making a Presentation at a colleague's Retirement Dinner? You may be presenting Sales Figures to your Team or convincing Management to provide funds for more Staff Training. Whatever the reason, we need to think about our audience ***first***, in order to prepare you for the task ahead.

So, what expectations do the members of an audience have of a speaker? Indeed what makes a good speaker? We need to look at Speaking in Public from the audience's perspective first, before we look at 'Delivery and Performance' techniques from the speaker's point of view. Professional Speakers always consider their listener's needs before their own, (just as a successful host will be considerate of a guest's needs first.)

Certainly we expect our speaker to look relaxed, sound confident and appear fully in control. We expect you to keep our interest. We expect you to be well prepared, choosing the right words, and spoken with an easy, natural delivery. Your audience doesn't want to watch you through gritted teeth, fully aware of what an ordeal it is for you.

Top Notch Speakers don't apologise, "I'm not very good at this", "I haven't done this before", "Unaccustomed as I am", "I haven't had time to prepare anything".

Over the past 20 years, I have listened to many well-penned speeches but unfortunately watched only a few memorable ***speakers***. I've listened intently, because I'm a Teacher and it's of great interest to me. However, I've witnessed many a bored, restless audience or a listless one with a glazed look in their eyes, who have politely sat through a speech delivered at a rate of knots, no eye contact made whatsoever and no thought given to connecting with them.

We have over the years lost our sensitivity to language, due to modern technology. It's a very visual world now and oral traditions such as storytelling and reading out aloud are no longer commonplace. We're so out of practice with getting up on our feet and communicating with an audience, that we have quite basic expectations of what makes a successful delivery. We're more than grateful to be up on our feet, reading fluently! Believe me, members of the audience are very grateful too not to be in your position; but unfortunately they still have high expectations from you. It could all be so much more satisfying for everyone, if only you knew what to do!

We worry about making a fool of ourselves. Because we are simply unaccustomed to speaking in public and feel out of our depth, we can mistakenly think that we can't do it. Yes, there are many books on the market regarding Presentation skills, but concentrating mainly on how to prepare your talk and scant information on how to ***deliver*** those words. As a Voice Coach, that's the aspect of my work that I focus on; the spoken word.

Speaking effectively is not just for the brave, talented few; but with the right information, everyone can improve their communication skills. Success does breed success and a well-delivered speech gives you such a sense of achievement, that you want to do more and more! Most people are far more capable than they think they are. Voice Coaches know how important the mind/body unity is and how we feel about ourselves affects the sound of our voice. How you 'think yourself in' to this whole subject of Public Speaking is the key. The right attitude is the foundation that we build on, to get you to our end-goal. 'Performance' is a subject shrouded in mystery. I must say though, everyone I've ever taught is amazed how uncomplicated the advice is. However the challenge is to actually apply the information, to swap one set of habits for another.

If you've recently made a presentation or delivered a talk you'll understand why I say that the pressure to sound interesting and confident, can be overwhelming. Perhaps you're naturally rather shy and reserved? And to make matters even worse, if you're a confident person in your professional life and really rather capable in your own field, you can feel overwhelmed by feelings of inadequacy and embarrassment. You don't like not being in control. You feel vulnerable admitting you can't do something.

Let me reassure you, it takes effort and courage to be thrust into the public arena and especially when so many of you haven't been taught how to deliver those words. Admittedly some people just don't want to be the centre of attraction with **ALL EYES ON YOU!** However, more and more of you in your professional life are having to get used to giving regular presentations. The bottom line is - you can only improve your presentation and speaking skills by speaking, so we're going to find other ways and means to practise before the actual event.

We're going to emulate the tactics and strategies that top-notch speakers adopt. Dynamic, charismatic speakers build up a rapport with their audience. They draw us in, compel us to hear their message. These speakers connect with their audience and allow us to be moved by their words. And so will you. Don't wait until you feel more confident as a person before you have a go at Public Speaking. The skills that you learn that will ***enable*** you to become more confident.

Let me explain; my husband has lived with a stammer, to a greater or lesser extent, all his life. At times, it has prevented him from taking on any form of Public Speaking. I began teaching and devising my 7 step programme and helped him apply the skills. Slowly but surely his confidence has grown and grown. He has become the most accomplished speaker now, taking on speaking roles that previously would have fazed him. He has learnt to speak from the heart, simple words spoken sincerely. His stammer re-emerges from time to time - so what; the audience is with him whilst he gets to grips with it or finds another word. He has become a relaxed, confident speaker, able to ad-lib, to joke and respond to his audience. His dry wit and his personality shines through. This is what captures your audience.

We need to foster feelings of self-esteem and self-worth. I want you to understand the process that dynamic speakers have developed. Let's think about how we use our voice in our daily lives. We do tend to put 'voice' into different compartments. A 'voice' we use to read the children a story. A 'voice' we use with close friends, perhaps talking about a holiday, or a recent film or something that really interests you. Now, think about the 'voice' you use at work. And the 'voice' you think you should use when speaking in front of an audience. You could be the Groom or the Bride's Father or the Best Man. You could be introducing a speaker or giving a vote of thanks or making a presentation to a business colleague.

When you feel comfortable in your environment, when you don't feel threatened by the unfamiliar situation that presents itself, then the voice sounds more natural and expressive. When we read out children's stories, we've given ourselves permission to lose our inhibitions and have some fun with characterisation. When we feel at ease, we intuitively atune ourselves to what our listener wants. If we go too fast, our child or children can't make sense of the words or the plot or the dialogue. And so it is with the rest of us too! We can't take in the words, their meaning, as quickly as you can say them! Think about how you sound, relating anecdotes to friends and family. Perhaps telling a joke. There's a to-ing and fro-ing between you and your listener. Eye contact and a silent acknowledgement that they're listening, perhaps a nodding of the head, a smile, a movement of the eyebrows. We relate to individuals. We need to view our audience as a unit of many individuals, not just a sea of faces. So you see, when you think about it, you are more capable of communicating and entertaining your audience than you thought.

Before we move onto the next step, Preparing Your Talk, I want you to make time to READ OUT ALOUD to any willing friend, spouse or colleague. Failing that, if you want to either surprise your friends, family or colleagues when you come to give your Presentation or Talk or just want the extra privacy, then get out your tape recorder! Read out articles, reports, after dinner stories, jokes, children's stories. Listen to your voice, do you race on, hardly pausing for the 'listener' to digest one idea before moving onto the next one? Are you expressive enough? Is your voice appropriate to what you are reading? Is it too formal, perhaps too business like for a less formal story? Don't forget in ordinary conversation, we're not really listening as intently as you do when you're sitting quietly listening to a speaker. We're more often than not distracted by what we want to say, in response to your words. Therefore, when speaking in Public you have a greater responsibility to make us feel comfortable, relaxed and interested in what you have to say.

Top-notch speakers know how important it is to match the sound of their voice to what they are saying. If you don't want to tape yourself, then enlist your trusted friend to give you some honest feedback. So vitally important! The more friends you can recruit the better. You need to get used to ALL EYES ON YOU - it's very unnerving at first but so necessary to go through the process so that you can get used to it! You'll be under the spotlight, under scrutiny, when delivering the real thing, so it's very important to have opportunities to have a dummy-run whenever possible. So please, be bothered to take on board this Reading Out Aloud exercise. It really is the basis of all our work. Any honest feedback will be valuable, even if it's not quite what you want to hear!

So ***enjoy*** the storytelling. Any positive comments will give you confidence. They'll always be room for improvement, so don't be too harsh on yourselves. We'll be covering all aspects of the

Spoken Word in the following steps. Develop a positive attitude. You can do it - everyone can become a more accomplished speaker if they have the right tools. Negative doubts and anxieties give rise to physical symptoms which clamp the voice. When you send out negative signals, perhaps speaking on a monotone or mumbling – you look unsure of yourself and will almost certainly feel inadequate. The mind controls the body. All you need to do is to apply these 7 Steps and you will conquer the fear of Speaking out in Public.

And, if you're a pretty confident person and you're not worried about getting up on your feet and saying a few words, as you do so quite regularly – I hope the following 'Trade Secrets' revealed here will help you to work on your Delivery Technique. Top-Notch Speakers are always willing to improve their skills; they're eager to learn more; they keep an open, flexible mind.

To sum up – Step 1 – The mind controls the body. The right attitude is vital for further work on the Performance Skills.

2 Preparing your talk

2 Preparing your talk

So many of you spend much time and effort in Preparing Your Talk. There are many excellent books on the market which delve into the whole process of structuring your talks, using personal anecdotes, quotations, etc. I'd like to bring to your attention a few points that I've found reoccur quite often. If it is at all possible - prepare well in advance - blind panic doesn't help you think clearly as you put pen to paper.

First of all, and it's all too easy to forget when writing your talk or Presentation, you need to ***write as you speak***. The audience doesn't want to be subjected to a spoken essay. When speaking to an audience we need to focus on the spoken word as opposed to the written. Every Top-notch or professional speaker has learnt to consider the needs of an audience. Try to use familiar vocabulary that you're used to. Yes, we are out to impress our audience with the words we've chosen but consider the following first. Match the words you use to the occasion. Don't use over-fussy or formal vocabulary in an informal speech and vice-versa. Perhaps at this point I should point out that it is not in everyone's best interest if the Best Man tells a rather risqué story about the Groom in front of older relatives. The Bride might not be too thrilled either!
Choose appropriate words and sentiments for the right audience.

Write your words from the heart - whether for a social or professional event. That's what makes your message memorable, that's what we take away with us. As you write, think about 'key' words or phrases that you want your audience to focus on. Underline those 'key' words. Think about how words create visual images. Make sure you can pronounce the words you choose. You don't want to lose credibility. Be careful with words you've only seen in print, but not heard. Be bothered to look at the pronunciation key in any good dictionary or CD ROM Dictionary with sound. Any 'faux pas' made in pronouncing a word incorrectly will stay with your audience long after your talk is finished. Don't compromise your credibility. These little 'slips' stay in the memory of those who want to score points against you, for a surprising long time.

Get used to the sound of your own voice. When practising, read your talk out ALOUD! Think about the words you have used, for example 'welcome', 'delighted', 'it's an honour, and privilege'. Say the words with expression in your voice, as if you mean it. Don't gloss over them. We're aiming to 'lift' the words off the page. If you can sound excited or enthusiastic about what you're saying, you're halfway there. Your aim is to build a rapport with your audience. Reach out to them, 'confide' in them and you'll draw them in. You have to make your audience listen to what you have to say. Be yourself - but one that is more animated, slightly 'larger than life'. Speak from the heart.

As we said earlier we've lost an element in today's visual, frenetic world, of **'listening'** - so we can so easily gloss over important key words such as 'welcome' and 'delighted'. We may register them in our minds when writing them down but forget to emphasise them or use any expression in our own voice to match the words. The 'spoken word' is friendlier, simpler, more emotive. Do use Onomatopoeia, Alliteration, Repetition and Figures of Speech for effect - all devices used by Top-notch speakers to speakers to enhance their message.

As you write, put yourself in the situation you're writing for. We want our audience to feel comfortable. A speaker who reads out his talk well, is much more successful than one, through lack of confidence or experience, dries up when faced with a few bullet points on cards. I would say in my opinion, thinking about the speeches I've heard over the past 20 years; don't be over ambitious at first, write everything out that you want to say - become adept at reading out. When you've become accomplished at this, when it becomes second nature, then you can move onto reading a few notes or bullet points written on cards.

When practising, (out aloud), underline those key words. We need to emphasise those words. Hold your script, elbows tucked into your side, so that we can see you as you read. Keep your head level as you read, we don't want to see the top of your head. We need to see your eyes. Think about the words you've written - SMILE at appropriate points. Let the words affect you, in turn they will affect your listeners. Start to think about getting your head out of the page - start with a key word - make ***eye contact***. Look at them! We do this in everyday conversation, don't we? We need this connection with our fellow human beings. Obviously in practise - your audience might very well be an imaginary one, or one person or even a small group of friends or colleagues.

Don't forget with a few bullet points on cards, you've got to be perfectly 'au fait' with your subject matter and confident enough and experienced enough to talk from notes. It's not for the beginner and I want you to taste success from your very next talk or Presentation. Being able to talk from notes (usually single trigger words) will come, as you become more self assured but it's not the be-all and end-all to becoming a Top-Notch Speaker. Reading out well is certainly a better option.

A word about ***Nerves!***

Once you've learnt all the secrets of Top-notch speakers - you'll feel that we've unravelled a subject that once seemed slightly out of reach. It'll no longer be an unknown quantity - for a gifted few. You won't need to feel worried or apprehensive. We'll be talking about 'nerves' quite a bit because it does have a knock-on effect throughout all the work that we'll cover. We can be nervous because we don't know what to expect, we're not prepared enough, we feel out of our depth. Your audience will react quite negatively to any overt signs of nervousness - wobbly voice, breathlessness, sweat on brows - you'll make them feel anxious and embarrassed. As I said to you before negative doubts give rise to physical symptoms, which will alter the sound of your voice and affect how those words are received.

Put your talk aside now and let's cover the Delivery Techniques of Body Language, Tone of Voice, Projection, Diction and Vocal Expression and you'll look at those words you've written in a different light.

3 Your Body Language

3 Your Body Language

Our first impression is a visual one!

We communicate using words, tone of voice, gestures, stance, eye contact and facial expression. We attach a greater significance to our words than perhaps we ought to. The truth is, we don't really understand the importance of our unspoken language.

The signals of non-verbal language, our 'body language' reveals more about our true feelings than we realise. When we feel nervous, apprehensive, out of control, we display signals such as fidgeting, pacing, repeated swallowing, wobbly voice (often heard on an answer phone), gazing at the ceiling or floor, fiddling with hair; all give-aways of our inner tension! I would say we can all identify with one of these!

Professional speakers have learned to mask those feelings and "leakage" of negative signals because they know they must appear to be and need to feel in control and make the audience feel comfortable. Try not to look so worried or preoccupied with the task in hand, which can result in frowning or scowling, as you feel weighed down with the enormity of it all.

By mimicking positive, open signals of confident speakers, we can eventually exchange one set of habits for another. Believe in what you say – otherwise they'll be no connection with your audience and a gradual weakening of eye contact.

Professional speakers display 'open' signals, wide shoulders, straight backs, heads balanced evenly on necks, arms by their side, unclenched fists, they'll smile (when it's appropriate) which will ensure unclenched teeth and jaws. They'll adopt steady eye contact from beginning to end. They'll know how important it is to develop a relationship with their audience – they'll work the room continuously, splitting the room into three or four sections (depending on size of room and audience) and giving each part equal attention. They want to be successful in what they do – so they make the effort to do it. 'Success makes you feel good!'. You'll come back for more.

Professional speakers understand what skills are needed to make their speech 'work'. They logically work out what an audience needs – a speaker who appears in control. So 'nerves' are dealt with - otherwise when we feel out of our depth we experience pounding hearts, dry mouth, sweating palms. Our stomach muscles tighten, as well as muscles in the back, shoulders and jaw. Our breathing becomes shallow; our lungs can't fill with air properly, as tension in the shoulder and back prevent the rib cage opening out. Tension transfers to the voice box, the larynx. We've all experienced that tell-tale lump in the throat sensation, when we feel we can't breathe. Our vocal range is limited. We can't project. Tension in the jaw restricts the movements of the lips, tongue and soft palate. The sound of the voice is harsh and shrill and the clarity of our words is affected. We can eliminate all these elements of nervousness by understanding what we are trying to achieve and why.

These 'negative' signals are very revealing and especially so, if there is a disparity between your body language and what you have to say. As language developed after our non-verbal communication, our primitive response is to trust the non-verbal signals. So we have to deal with any negative doubts about our ability to get up there and relate to our audience. Worrying about how prepared we are, how accomplished we feel, what image are we conveying – all have to be dealt with 'pre-performance' – otherwise we'll display lowered heads and eye gaze, hunched shoulders, dry mouths, shaking hands, sweating brows. We may not see your pounding heart – but we'll certainly hear it!

Practice – getting up on your feet, walk to the table or lectern. Practice smiling, looking around the room; imagine your audience. Confident, self-assured people own more 'space' – they take up more room. Watch yourself in every window, every mirror whilst you're adopting the habits of successful speakers. These 'open' signals are the building blocks you need before we can move onto voice work. Notice if you clench your fists whilst out window shopping. When you're stuck in a traffic jam or queuing at the supermarket, are you clenching your teeth and jaw? We need to be aware of these habits and try to get rid of them before we find ourselves displaying these negative signals as we get up to speak.

Enlist your friend, spouse or colleague to monitor you and give you feedback. Your posture equals your image. Confident people convey status via their body language.

Your ***stance*** when speaking should be, feet evenly balanced, hip distance apart. Shoulders should sit low and down into your back – they don't belong up by your ears!
Heads evenly balanced (they weigh approximately 1 stone or 7kg) on your necks. Be aware of any distracting mannerisms swaying, sniffing (yes, sniffing!), hopping from one foot to another. Keep still! Try to become a little more introspective as you take on board these skills - as I've found most people have no idea that they have these mannerisms!

Think about a natural, easy body alignment – head, neck, spine and pelvis in alignment. We're aiming for a relaxed stance, a speaker who looks in control and happy to be there.

Let the words affect you, as they do whilst talking to friends. Facial expression is vital for successful communication. However, facial expression can't be superimposed. It develops naturally when you feel confident about what you are saying; you react to the sentiments expressed and this in turn is registered on your face. We often look quite animated whilst speaking on the phone, when we can't be seen! Put many people in front of an audience though and they'll clam up, their faces suddenly registering a blank expression – very off-putting. Eye contact is also vital and it has to be CONTACT with your audience, not a token quick flick of the eyes. We hopefully and usually look at people whilst speaking to them during normal conversation but put us in front of an audience and we become a different person. That's why your trusted group of friends or family who will monitor you and give you feedback are so important to this whole process.

When do we make eye contact? First of all, before you start to speak look around and make eye contact with your audience; then as you start to speak; at key words you want to emphasise; look up at your audience at beginning of paragraphs (a new idea or point of view); and as you end your talk, slow down and make this connection. A script is a barrier between us and our audience, so we need to get our heads out of it as often as possible! Talking from bullet points takes a great deal of experience and a thorough knowledge of your subject (but the advantage is that you're looking at your audience all the time).

SMILE when you can – it changes the sound of your voice. Don't just think happy thoughts! When reading out – keep your head level, don't bury your head in your talk with chin and eyes down. We desperately need to see your face and eyes so don't hold your notes too high, hiding your face. Keep your elbows tucked into your sides as you hold your script, notes or cards.

Mimic the unspoken signals of a confident speaker. Open, relaxed gestures. The front of the body is exposed, rather than closed positions such as wrapping arms across your body. When sitting, don't slump or cross legs; the signals you are sending out suggest you are protecting yourself or reassuring yourself. Remember you are under the microscope before you reach the rostrum or lectern. Once you have been allotted the title 'speaker' – you'll be under scrutiny before, during and after your talk. Be careful with distracting repetitive mannerisms.

Top-Notch Speakers do not allow any 'leakage' of gestures that show any discomfort. i.e. clenched fists, set jaws, body grooming – stroking arms, hair, rubbing the tops of your thumb nails, sifting through notes, jingling change or keys in your pocket, clicking pen tops, taking glasses on and off, swaying from one foot to the other. Uneasiness is also conveyed by a shift of the whole body, usually more noticeable when sitting down. So take note when going for that important interview! Don't give anything away to alert us to your inner tension. You've lost your audience by then – they've stopped listening and are focused on looking out for those repetitive displays of nervousness.

Memorise this: if you act as though you are confident, strangely enough people respond to you as though you are and this in turn will make you feel more confident!

4 Tone of Voice

4 Tone of Voice

More hurt feelings are caused by using the wrong 'tone of voice' than most people realise. The tone of voice you adopt in reality is how your message is received by your audience rather than the actual words used. We should strive to match our tone of voice to the occasion and the words we use. Top-notch speakers do.
If there is a disparity between how we sound and what we say, our primitive instinct is to trust the sound of the voice, as words came after our non-verbal language in the development of our communications skills.

How do you want to come across? Lively, enthusiastic, serious? When we feel out of control, nervous, apprehensive, this can have a direct effect on the sound of our voice. Our body changes shape, and therefore our breathing is affected. Our breathing pattern changes to how we feel. The muscles involved in making our voice will tighten and the result will be a harsher, shriller sound. The voice is a precise mood indicator. The ear is very sensitive. We are de-coding non-verbal signals more than we realise.

So, onto some exercises now to relax the body and mind and ensure a more open resonant sound. After all – as a Public Speaker you want to affect your audience by what you have to say. We are moved by words. Confident, professional speakers have learnt this fact and apply it over and over again.

Tiredness and stress effect the way we feel, our posture, our breathing rhythms and consequently how we sound.

As obvious as it may seem, it helps if you open your mouth wide enough when speaking! I do think there is an inbuilt reluctance to open the mouth too wide as it conjures up images of being too loud, maybe appearing a bit brash, or overly confident; so we may need some extra effort from you to put this into practice. Think about this one, when you want to sound animated and friendly SMILE as you say the words. Actors on the radio and T.V. do so when advertising products and cajoling you to buy! Top-notch speakers do it!

Have a go – but you need to actually smile as you speak, not just thinking pleasant thoughts! Technically speaking, this works because the throat and mouth widens when smiling, the jaw is relaxed and open and the sound waves reverberate in your throat and mouth (as in a cave!).

Firstly we need to check our posture and body alignment. The head – neck – back – pelvis alignment affect the positioning of our rib-cage, and so consequently the shape of our lungs and the amount of air taken in. This is the major influence regarding our tone of voice. It follows then that we have to look for ways to release unnecessary tension in the body because tension, either physical or emotional, tightens the vocal tract (comprising the neck, jaw, mouth, tongue and soft palate) and makes the voice sound harsh.

We can all hear tension say in friends voices, on the phone, when we can't see the caller but are certainly aware of and affected by the differing tone of voice. Emotional tension is dealt with in Step 1 and 2 when we've considered our attitude to getting up to say say a few words and making sure we are akin to what an audience expects from a speaker and how to write your talk accordingly. Tension can be shown by a constant stream of er's, um's, you know's. Rely on your friend or colleague to alert you to these – you'd be surprised how many people don't realise they do this.

Stand up, feet hip distance apart, think about the head, neck, shoulder, back and pelvis alignment. Aim for a relaxed posture. When our shoulders are relaxed and held down and wide, the larynx (voice box) sits lower in our neck and this has a direct affect on the sound of our voice. Our posture is affected by stress and tension.

So, now line up against the edge of a door! Keep your head steady, balanced on your neck, neither too forward or back. Remember it weighs approximately 1 stone (7 kg)! There are two natural curves, one in the neck and the other in the small of the back. Unlock your knees. Unclench your fists! Unclench your jaw! Now, walk away and stand in this position. Imagine a cord is pulling your body position upwards. Become aware of a sense of length in the back of your neck and spine. Keep the shoulders, the shoulder blades down, they should rest low and wide, they don't belong by your ears! Have a good stretch, really stretch your body. This is a basic Alexander Technique exercise. Briefly, Frederick Mattias Alexander was an actor who found out through mis-use of his body that the power of his voice was affected. He developed his technique, and it has been adopted worldwide by everyone concerned with correcting the imbalances of the body which are reflected in the sound of our voice, along with the holistic viewpoint that the mind and body are essentially one.

Have a good old yawn – this really opens up your throat and loosens the jaw. Clench and unclench your teeth – this relaxes the jaw too. Raise shoulders to ears, hold and release. Roll your shoulders forward, back and alternately. Tilt head gently forward, back, side to side. Chin to chest and return to the centre. Look over alternate shoulders, hold and stretch. Relax the back of the neck by gently nodding and lengthening it out.

Sit down now. Aim for an alert posture. Think about the back of the chair supporting your back. Keep the same balanced head, neck, back alignment as you did when standing. Think about that cord pulling upwards from the top of your head. Uncross legs, otherwise your rib-cage will be narrowed and this affects the sound of your voice. Avoid sitting forward, with slumped back. Keep a sense of lengthening in the back of your neck and spine. Gently nod your head to release tension. We need to develop and learn a different set of habits now. You will feel more energised and look more alert and therefore sound more confident.

It is vital to mimic the sense of openness in the head, neck, shoulder area because this has a direct bearing on how we breathe. Our breath is the energy source for the voice, ensuring that the voice can resonate and has enough fuel to project the voice. Breathe out a whispered 'ah' sound – do this especially when you feel 'nervous' (ideally, find a quiet and private 'space').
This opens up the jaw and throat. Breath deeply and rhythmically into the centre of your body. The abdominal muscles will automatically be engaged. We need this support of the muscles for the voice to carry. When we breathe from the abdomen, more oxygen is forced into the lungs. You'll sound calmer. They'll be more energy in your voice.
More oxygen in the bloodstream equals a reduction of your stress levels, blood pressure, heart rate. When we're stressed or adopting the wrong posture, our breathing pattern shifts into the upper part of the body. The result us a shriller, less powerful, less resonant voice.

Stand up now. Breathe in. Let your stomach relax (it should protrude a little). Think about taking breath into the body, let the body swell a little with the extra air intake. Feel expansion in your midriff area, waist and back. Keep your shoulders relaxed and down.

Breath out. We speak on the out-going flow of air. As you breath out, become aware of pulling the stomach in. Visualise taking breath out of the body. Think about wanting to share words, projecting them out of your mouth to your listeners.

As muscles contract, imagine pushing gently the column of air from your stomach up towards your neck and mouth. Imagine an open throat and mouth.

Repeat with the sound "ah" now, but not whispering. Make it louder. Again, even louder. Pull in the abdominal muscles even more. Don't be tempted as you become louder to push the sound out using movements of the neck and head, as if pushing the sound out. We can do this so easily! Beware. You'll make the sound strident. This neck and head movement makes the neck tight and closes the throat, tensing the back of the tongue and soft palate.

Keep the jaw relaxed and open. Tap the tongue tip against the hard ridge behind the top front teeth. Make light quick tapping movements, sound out the t and d sounds, as in the words top and dog. Release any tension in the back of the tongue and soft palate, making k and g sounds, as in the words kick and goal. Breathe out, let the breath come back into your body of its own accord (it's a natural reflex action). When you're ready say "Good Evening, Ladies and Gentlemen" Breathe "I'd like to introduce our keynote speaker Gillian Cohen" Breathe "Who is going to reveal the secrets of Top-Notch Speakers". Breathe.

We should aim to regulate our breathing with what we have to say. The deep and rhythmical breathing ensures a smooth flow of words. Ends of sentences don't fade away. It helps alleviate pounding hearts when feeling nervous and unsure of oneself. Be aware also that when we're nervous we often talk far too quickly, we forget to take extra breath and as we start to run out of breath the voice trails off at the ends of sentences. Match your breathing to the phrasing you use. We only really become aware of our breathing when it becomes difficult, for example when climbing a long flight of stairs. Deep centred breathing is healthier for us, is a natural way of breathing and will make us feel more lively and positive.

To sum up, your tone of voice equals your message to your audience. Achieve this by adopting the right body alignment, releasing unnecessary tension both emotionally and physically and developing a more centred method of breathing. This is the foundation work for voice which we can build on.

5 Projection

5 Projection

Too many of you worry unnecessarily about whether your voice will 'project' enough to your audience. We actually project our voices instinctively when we are committed to what we have to say and eager to connect with our audience. Projection is not so much about volume, how loud you are (though you do want to be heard) but more to do with your willingness and intention to reach out to your audience. In fact, too much emphasis on people telling you to 'speak up' can often have a detrimental effect as you could be tempted to raise your head and thrust your chin out. Your voice can become less clear because you are concentrating on being louder and maybe even start to shout, and therefore the inflections in the voice, which denote meaning and variety, are ironed out.

Your audience needs to be moved by your words and the feelings expressed. Every top-notch speaker draws you in, you are affected by what they have to say and their ability to create a rapport with you. Their words are matched by vocal expression, coupled with the right facial expression and gestures. Think about this – we 'mentally' project our voices to make sure we are heard when we want to be heard. Think about occasions when we feel irate or passionate about a point of view you want to get across. You're not worried about being the centre of attention for those few moments or bothered about all eyes on you! You're focused on getting your point across. Feeling confident about your subject

matter, what you have to say, allows you to relax and start the process of reaching out to your listener.
'Delivery' or 'Performance' techniques are the tools to enable you to do this.

As I mentioned before, make sure you open your mouth wide enough as you speak, so that you don't trap the sound in. If you're not loud enough, could it be that you're not really committed enough to what you are saying?
Check that you're not clenching your teeth. A tip worth knowing; imagine you're holding a grain of rice between your teeth (in repose – when not actually speaking). This keeps the lips slightly open and stops your face looking too set.

A dehydrated voice won't be able to project as the vocal mechanism can't work efficiently and it will also lack resonance. Make sure you're drinking plenty of water as opposed to tea, coffee and cola drinks which act as a diuretic. Make sure that you're not losing moisture through perspiration, whether through nerves, being too hot because either you're dressed too warmly or the room's too hot. A dry throat sounds tight, can't resonate properly, and the intonation of your voice will be affected too.

When you're dehydrated you can feel quite unwell, have a throbbing head, feel lethargic and not able to think clearly at all.

All this you can mistakenly attribute to having to get up on your feet and speak out! If you've got a cold, be careful with any medication that offers to dry up your cold, it will dry up your vocal tract too and your voice will be affected.

A dry throat and mouth can often be a signal to the brain that you are nervous. When nervous your breathing pattern will therefore alter, the larynx (voice box) rises and your vocal cords tighten. The pitch of your voice rises and the resultant sound will be shriller and tense. Keep hydrated and mimic the habits of professional speakers!

If you know that you 'mumble' when hurled up on your feet to speak, ask yourself a couple of questions first. Are you sure you are committed to what you've written? Has somebody else written your speech? Perhaps you're still rather shy underneath the required bravado you feel you need for Public Speaking and rather worried about your task ahead. Maybe you're just not used to people watching and listening to you. If you're quite a quiet person, you know that more extrovert people tend to take over, hog the limelight. As adults anyway, we tend to become more inhibited in how we use our voices compared to our childhood.

You need to project your voice using your abdominal muscles. Don't try to push your voice from the throat; otherwise you could end up coughing and spluttering as you try to turn up the volume.

Remember to keep your shoulders down, head, neck, back and pelvis in alignment. 'Speak out' to your audience. We want to make sure that your voice retains its warmth and vitality. If you push your voice you can cancel out many of your inflections and intonation. Also, don't be tempted to grip the sides of the lectern or table in the hope that this will help you propel the sound out, if you haven't got the use of a microphone.

It's vitally important here to re-consider your words and the phrasing you've used. Use your breath support to match what you're saying.

For example: ' I'd like to welcome you all this evening ' – can be said on one breath rather then chopped up into too many phrases.

' I'd like to | welcome | you all | here | this evening '

but it does require more energy and use of your stomach muscles to get that sound across to your listeners. Don't forget to make eye contact, work the room and use facial expression and gestures.

Here's an exercise to strengthen your abdominal muscles.

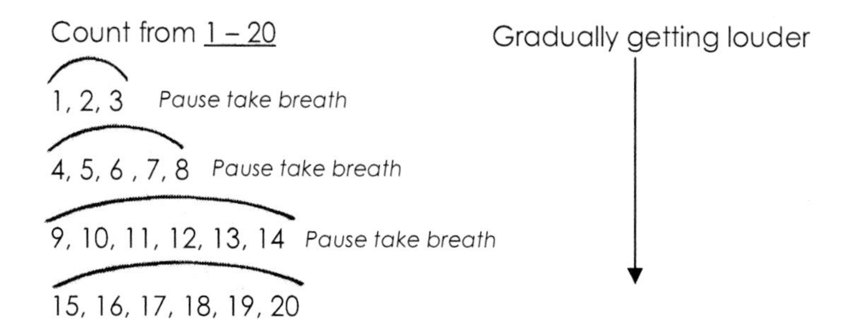

Repeat, count from 1 – 10 on one breath.
Pause, take breath count from 11 – 20.
gradually getting louder. You need more fuel, more energy (breath) as you become louder and speak for longer.

Keep your shoulders down, concentrate on working your abdominals, breathe in, stomach out, breathe out, stomach in (the opposite to how most people were taught at school!). A useful exercise to do whilst out walking. Keep yourself reasonably fit for voice work; you'll feel more energised, with more oxygen getting into your bloodstream, your stomach muscles will become more toned. Visualise drawing air into the body, your stomach wall swells; air out of the body, engage the abdominals. As more oxygen in the body makes you feel more vibrant and lively, **guess how you'll sound?!**

The Microphone

Firstly, don't rely on yours to work! Try to have a practice before you start your speech. Get used to the sound of your voice coming out of the microphone. It sounds different. Obviously, if your microphone works, then don't focus on projecting your voice so much. Speak at your usual volume level.

Be careful you don't move about, thereby going off Microphone, if yours is fixed on the desk, rather than a lapel or hand-held one, otherwise your voice will sound in and out as the Microphone picks you up intermittently. Practice so that you can cope without one. Ask for a friend's or colleague's opinion on how you sound. Project your voice to the back of the room. If your microphone fails you whilst you're speaking, you won't be fazed and can carry on. This will win you major points. Allow extra time for this. Remember, if you're busy with a microphone in one hand, what do you do with your notes? How do you turn over the pages? This needs practice; so practice beforehand with a prop in your hand.

Realistically, most people won't be able to practice with a microphone, until just before their event. If things go wrong then, it can unnerve you for the task ahead. You want to sound 'normal' but be aware that many people react quite strangely to the sound by their voice coming out of a Microphone – and dealing with this takes up time, valuable run-through time. You also have to be determined to perform your speech as you have so far, in rehearsal, rather than becoming distracted by the voice that you put on for the Microphone! When you're holding a Microphone some people start to over-act, others become inhibited. Allow enough time to adjust to this; you'll calm down and be ready to go.

To sum up – **Insist** you have a practice – but once you have mastered the technique, a microphone is a very useful aid.

Projection, as I said earlier, is all about committing yourself to your words. ***Concentrate*** on what you are saying, don't be tempted to gloss over words and their meaning, the sentiments expressed, possibly because you've become over–familiar with the words on the page. Perhaps you've been trying to memorise parts of your speech and the words now seem out of your grasp. **Top-Notch speakers never learn a speech word for word.** I know actors do it – but that is a different technique. By all means, learn your opening line and be able to look at your audience as you say it – but a definite no to memorising chunks of a speech. Don't be distracted either by members of the audience, or other thoughts on your mind – remember, **you have a job to do** – so keep focused – otherwise your audience will react negatively to this and switch off.

Make sure your words are clear; we'll be covering Diction and Pronunciation in the next Step.

Some exercises for you; to become more aware of muscularity of the lips and tongue.

- Smile an exaggerated smile! Pucker your lips, stretch them back. Blow through your lips. Vibrate them as if you're really cold – br, br, br!
- Chew an imaginary sticky toffee, use your tongue to pick it off your teeth.
- Tap your tongue against the hard palate (the gum ridge behind your front teeth) – t, d, l, n - let those sounds really reverberate.
- Exaggerate the lip sounds p, b, w, m, f, v – feel the vibrations.
- Exercise the soft palate at the back of the mouth k, g, ng - ah. (ng – as in the word su<u>ng</u>)

Notice that when people are skilled in any physical activity, they have learned to use their muscles in a relaxed and efficient manner. Better muscular skill in speaking means greater audibility.

Visual Aids

Many books discuss in great detail the use of visual aids. Through my own experience in delivering Staff Training Workshops and Presentations, I would like to add this – technology can let you down; always have Plan B in mind! OHP's and 'Computer Presentation' are not infallible. A Flipchart, where you've written or displayed Bullet Points, Diagrams, Statistics can be a more reliable option. However, **you** are your best Visual Aid! They are there to help you, to enhance your presentation – not the other way round.

6 How Now Brown Cow and all that.....

6 How Now Brown Cow and all that...

Hands up how many hackles rose as you read the title of this section! Or not, for those of you who are concerned with how you sound, and how you pronounce words.

And to be even more controversial - does accent matter these days? (I know it's not P.C. to talk about this any more!) I would say – if it matters to you then yes, your accent does matter and it's your prerogative to do something about it if you want to! I have to say that some voices are easier to listen to than others from a Public Speaking viewpoint, as the words are clearer and project more easily. If our work and social life never takes us beyond our home environment then it really doesn't matter; our ears are attuned to those familiar speech patterns. It only becomes an issue as we move away from our home base and perhaps want to fit in and blend in with those around us. It's a natural reaction; a basic instinct, to be part of a social group with similar speech 'tunes'.

The subject of 'accent' is still bound up with 'elocution' which fell out of favour probably some forty years ago. At that time 'elocution' was seen as divisive, elitist, old-fashioned and an artificial, super-imposed way of speaking. Here is my advice from meeting and teaching many people over a twenty year span. We can't deny that we do have a 'category' of speech known as 'Standard Speech' or R.P. (Received Pronunciation) – check out the definition and Pronunciation key in any dictionary. We use 'Standard Speech' as a baseline to work from. It's become quite ridiculous that we almost can't acknowledge publicly that R.P. exists; privately though, it's a very different matter. Many of you want to speak with a more international 'neutral' voice that fits in and is easily understood all over the English-Speaking world.

If you are interested in learning this accent (actors have to) that is your choice. How you reached your decision is your business and you are perfectly entitled to seek help from a Voice Coach who is trained in phonetics and dialects. Be prepared for some criticism though, nothing stirs people up quite as much as a discussion on 'accents'!

However, if you choose to adopt 'standard' speech sounds (usually referred to as BBC English) then at least **be consistent**. For example, don't have some words with a short 'a' sound as in the word gather and others with a long 'ah' sound as in the word glass and substitute one for the other. You will lose credibility. Listen carefully to those people whose voice and speech you'd like to emulate. We do this quite happily in other areas of our lives and aren't criticised for it. With voice – we are touching a basic, primeval raw nerve here and if you sound as if your accent is put on, fake, sending out signals that you're pretending to be something you're not – then I'm afraid your listeners will react negatively to this and turn off. The subject of accent is bound up with 'class', status, education; some people feel you shouldn't be disloyal to your upbringing and natural dialect, by wanting to sound different. However, in a free society – we must be allowed to decide for ourselves. But **remember** be consistent, otherwise you'll make a fool of yourself.

Check out words in a dictionary. These days most of them have a pronunciation guide that's easy to follow or listen to a CD ROM Dictionary with sound. Make sure you can pronounce words you haven't heard, which you've only seen in print before. We tend to, quite understandably, make an effort to impress others when we get up on our feet to speak out and could be tempted to use unfamiliar or more complex words. Make the effort to double-check their pronunciation for the world out there is a merciless place and a 'faux pas' made in how you say the words will stay with you long after your speech is a distant memory.

Language skills develop during our formative years. We imitate sounds as children this is why family members often sound alike with the same stress patterns on words and the same intonation.

If you are going to be in the position of getting up on your feet to speak out in front of an audience, (whichever accent you choose) make sure that your speech is at least clear. We make our speech sounds using the muscles of the lips, tongue and soft palate. These muscles need to be exercised. I list for your convenience all the consonant sounds that we make. Many people are amazed how muffled their speech can be if they're not making the sounds clearly. This will also help you project more easily.

If English is not your first Language, you may find the following particularly helpful, as many talented, ambitious, qualified professionals feel they are held back due to a lack of confidence in their Spoken English Skills.

Many factors make up the 'speech tune' of a language – firstly, how the sounds are actually formed; the stress patterns on the syllables, the length of vowel sounds and the inflections in our voice.

Let's look at how the **consonant** sounds are formed.

Sounds made primarily by the **LIPS**, are:

p as in pin
b as in bin — Lips together and part

f as in fit
v as in very — Top teeth connects with the bottom lip

r as in road — Lips forward, made with the front of the tongue curled up slightly and sound released against teeth ridge.

m as in meat — Lips together, the soft palate is lowered and the sound escapes through the nose.

w as in weed — Lips forward and rounded, back of tongue is raised.

make sure these 'fronting' sounds are made at the front of the mouth as this helps also with resonance and projection.

Sounds made primarily by the **TONGUE** are:

t as in tin
d as in day — The tongue tip touches the hard palate (the ridge behind your front teeth) is held and released.

s as in sat
z as in zoo — The tip of the tongue is pressed against the teeth – the sound escapes down the channel in the centre of the tongue.

sh as in shoe zh as in vision	The sides of the tongue are pressed against the gums and the tongue is arched high to make pressure between it and the roof of the mouth.
ch as in chair j as in judge	The closing of the jaw and the tongue pressed against the teeth and hard palate and then released.
tr as in tree dr as in dream	The centre of the tongue is hollowed, ready for the 'r' friction
l as in lettuce	the tip of the tongue against the gum ridge behind the top front teeth, sides of the tongue lowered allowing the sound to escape out of the mouth.
n as in no	made by the tongue tip pressed against the gum ridge, the soft palate is lowered and the sound escapes through the nose.
th as in mouth th as in there	Tongue tip is held just behind the upper front teeth, which are open slightly, friction is created between the teeth and the tongue tip.
y as in yes	tongue held against hard palate, forward lips.
h as in happy	tongue blade raised at the back of the mouth, air forced through.

Sounds made primarily by the **SOFT PALATE** are:

k as in kettle g as in girl	Back of tongue connects with the soft palate (continuation of the roof of your mouth – the soft fleshy part)
ng as in song	the back of the tongue connects with the lowered soft palate, sound escapes through the nose.

In order for your speech to be heard, make sure you sound your word beginnings and endings. Don't be tempted to gabble in order to get the ordeal over and done with! For whatever reason, you're up there on your feet – so rise to the occasion and make the best of it.

If you know you 'mumble' make sure this isn't due to the fact that you're not making the sounds firmly enough for your voice to carry. Er's and and um's and you know's need to be acknowledged and dealt with. It takes time and application to substitute a pause, SILENCE, where once you had a succession of those sound fillers. Sometimes you're not even aware you're making lots of um's, er's and 'you know what I mean' 's. Your friend or colleague whose opinion you value needs to relied upon to listen out for them and help you get rid of them, (or your tape recorder – which will at least help you become aware of them.)

Tongue Twisters are a useful way to exercise your speech muscles. Start off slowly and deliberately, emphasising the consonant sounds and then build up speed. Say them in a sequence of 3.

For the lips -

'A big bug bit a bold bald bear and the bold bald bear bled blood badly' and 'Three free flags'.

For the Tongue Tip -

'Does double bubble gum double bubble?'
and 'She sells sea-shells on the sea shore'.

For the soft palate and back of tongue

'Keenly cleaning copper kettles'
and 'The young singer was singing the wrong song'.

Better muscular skill in speaking means greater audibility. Unclench your teeth – keep your jaw relaxed and open. Your tongue should lie on the bottom of your mouth (when in repose and not actually speaking!), not tensed and raised to the roof of your mouth.

When you want to project it's harder to hear you if the words are distorted. Here are some frequent mis-pronunciations that I've come across.

- Substitutions

One consonant sound is substituted for another,

For example

Three	becomes	free
Thunder	becomes	Funder
Tuesday	becomes	Chewsday
Duke	becomes	Juke

- Distortions

Vowels become distorted,

For example

Day	becomes	die
Time	becomes	Toim
Again	becomes	agayn *(should be agen)*
Mountain	becomes	Mountayn *(should be Mounten)*
Party	becomes	Partee
City	becomes	Citee

Consonants become distorted

the idea of	becomes	idea rof
drawing room	becomes	drawring room
saw all	becomes	saw rall
awe inspiring	becomes	awe rinspiring
so easy	becomes	so weasy
who is	becomes	who wis
to improve	becomes	to wimprove
my eyes	becomes	my yeyes
my ears	becomes	my years
see all	becomes	see yall
my idea	becomes	my yidea
not at all	becomes	not tat tall
that's tough	becomes	that stuff

- Omissions

When syllables are dropped, it's much harder to hear you.

For example

it's hoh	for	it's hot
I'm gunna	for	I'm going to
buh	for	but
dah of bir	for	date of birth
gerrof	for	get off

- Additions

Extra syllables are often added,
For example

film	becomes	fillim
trembling	becomes	tremberling
didn't	becomes	diddunt
bottle	becomes	bott-tul
little	becomes	litt-tul
kettle	becomes	kett-tul
model	becomes	mod-dul
cotton	becomes	cott-ton
button	becomes	butt-ton
English	becomes	Engerlish
assembly	becomes	assemberly

The ***vowel*** sounds create the tone of our voice. The variations in these sounds is the dominant factor relating to our differing accents and dialects.

I list for you the 'standard' English vowel sounds. Some sounds are made predominantly by the ***lips*** and some by the ***tongue***. Some sounds are ***short-sounding*** and some are ***long-sounding***.

LIP VOWELS - the **lips predominantly** shape the sounds, going from a small firm circle to lips fully open.

OO	as in choose	Long Sound
oo	as in book	Short Sound
AW	as in saw	Long Sound
o	as in shot	Short Sound
OH	as in go	Long Sound
OW	as in house	Long Sound

OI	as in boy	Long Sound
OOR	as in pure	Long Sound
OH-ER	as in slower	Long Sound
OW-ER	as in flower	Long Sound
OI-ER	as in lawyer	Long Sound

TONGUE VOWELS – **the tongue predominantly** shapes the sounds. Lip shape is in a 'neutral' position, (which means they don't extend beyond their natural shape.) If you're interested – the tongue changes shape from a flat position to gradually arching upwards at the front of the mouth!

AH	as in mark	Long Sound
u	as in lunch	Short Sound
ER	as in learn	Long Sound
er	as in father	Short Sound
a	as in cat	Short Sound
e	as in bed	Short Sound
i	as in think	Short Sound
EE	as in see	Long Sound
AY	as in day	Long Sound
I	as in sky	Long Sound
EAR	as in pier	Long Sound
AIR	as in hair	Long Sound
AY-er	as in layer	Long Sound
I-er	as in fire	Long Sound

The most common difficulties for English Speakers (where English is not your first language) is substituting short sounds for long sounds. In many regional vowel sounds we would also substitute Tongue

Vowels for Lip Vowels, for example, the words lunch, butter, dull. I hope this overall view gives you a starting point, something to work from, if 'Standard English' Speech is something that interests you and you want to investigate further.

Glottal Stop

There's also much debate in the newspapers these days about the demise of our English language and the frequent occurrence of the Glottal Stop! There's a familiar staccato click at the beginning of a sound, usually a vowel sound; such as and often, in as the vocal cords are forced together.

However, if you're going to stand up and project for all it's worth, it follows that your speech should sound clear.

With the 'glottal stop', syllables are dropped.

For example

letter	becomes	le-er
people	becomes	peo-le
talking	becomes	ta-in
piano	becomes	pi-ano
water	becomes	wa-er

there is actually a – pause – literally a stop – between one syllable and another. There is technically a stoppage between the vocal cords and the glottis (the space at the top of the windpipe).

If you want to correct this, we need to look at how words are formed and pronounced in Standard English.

Every word in our language has a beat, a rhythm.
For instance, the word 'book' has one beat, one syllable. The word 'reading' has two beats, two syllables. 'Discussion' has three, 'television' has four and 'communication' has five syllables.
Every word that has more than one syllable has a main (primary) stress (usually the first syllable). This gives a word its tune, its rhythm. We can make a general rule, nouns have their main stress on the first syllable, verbs on the second syllable. **This is actually the key to Pronunciation.**

You have to re-learn how those words are formed. Of course, this is assuming that you are ***aware*** you're making these sound distortions. Your friend, colleague or tape recorder will be invaluable here. You may need extra work with a Voice Coach.

A 'Lisp'

Many people have come to me over the years to try to get rid of a 'lisp' – (whereby the sounds 'th' and 's', 'z', 't' and 'd' and 'f' and 'v' are substituted and distorted.) – as they feel the manner in which they speak over-rides what they have to say.

Look at the previous descriptions for how we make those sounds. In reality it isn't that the sounds can't be made in isolation but the patterns of speech have been laid down since childhood days and the difficulty lies in re-learning new habits.

Speech is made up of connected sounds, so we're always going from one sound to another to form our words. For example, the word 'pen', the lips come together for the 'p' sound, the 'e' is an open vowel sound, the 'n' sound tongue tip held against the gum ridge behind the top front teeth. Three sounds connected together to make the word 'pen'. With a 'lisp' the 'th' sound replaces the accepted sound we expect to hear, for instance 'pensive'. P-E-N (as above) but a 'th' sound (tongue tip resting behind slightly open teeth) is substituted for the 's' sound; so it becomes pen-thive. Some habits are more ingrained than others. You may need extra work with a Voice Coach here.

If you feel you want to have more personal tuition, you should consult a qualified and experienced teacher. Please refer to the recommended Professional bodies and their websites given at the end of the book!

7 Speech 'colour'

7 Speech 'colour'

When we speak with 'EXPRESSION' in the voice this is actually how our message connects to our audience. Many of you worry about speaking on a 'monotone' and I know are made aware of this particularly on an answer-phone recording.
In this section we're going to cover the why's and wherefore's – the tools that ensure we can deliver those words effectively, every single time.

The voice can be flat, lacking in energy; due to a lack of preparation, being preoccupied and distracted by the seemingly enormous task ahead of you (which can seem insurmountable). We can speak on one level due to nervousness. We can tend to 'drone' on because we feel self-conscious. To be able to 'speak from the heart' in public and to express yourself with ease is one of the greatest gifts a lucky few have naturally. Perhaps they grew up in a gregarious chatty family and these skills became second nature. However, all these skills can be taught and learnt. We're now going to concentrate on devices such as pitch, pace, pause and inflection to ensure that you too can become an accomplished speaker.

We do make judgments (unfairly) about a person from the way they speak. If their voice is flat and on one tone, perhaps we wrongly deduce that they aren't worth listening to because they won't have anything interesting to say. The inflections or intonation of the voice all add variety and meaning to our speech. The pitch changes (usually upwards) on key words emphasise those words. Usually they are accompanied by relevant facial expression and gestures too. We must make sure that our speech muscles (the tongue, lips, soft palate) are hydrated – speaking is very dehydrating and we need plenty of water for the vocal mechanism to work properly.

For example if we express "it's so wonderful to see so many of you here this evening" we change the pitch of the voice upwards on the word 'wonderful' to emphasise the word.

Variety of pace adds interest too. Slow down on important key words, as well as raising the pitch. Overall we shouldn't adopt too fast a pace nor one that's too slow. Remember though to match your pace to what you're saying – for example 'I'm so excited' if said too slowly, could sound rather sarcastic!

Raise the pitch of your voice at the start of a new paragraph, a new idea. This energises the voice and keeps the audience involved. Our aim is to engage our audience and then keep their attention!

Pause points help you pace your talk too. Pause at the end of a sentence – either snatch some breath or take a longer breath. Pauses allow your audience time to take in the words. We can speak so much faster than we can digest what is being said.
Hold your pause longer at the end of a paragraph before moving onto the next item. Enlist your trusted friend again as we cannot judge the length of a pause on our own.
I'm now going to cover each aspect of vocal expression in more detail.

When you listen to your voice, either on an answer phone message or if you've recorded yourselves reading out aloud – listen out for the phrasing you use, the emphasis, the pauses, the speed (pace), the pitch of the voice and the inflections in the voice which all communicate meaning.

We speak in phrases for example

'I'm going to take my umbrella, in case it rains.'
(two phrases in one sentence.)
A phrase can be a complete sentence. Read ahead to take in the phrasing when you read out aloud.

Pitch

The height and depth of our voice which actually means the expressiveness and vitality we can inject into our words. We usually use middle pitch for our conversational tone.

'Higher' pitch for excitement, happiness.

'Lower' pitch for more serious or thoughtful words.

- Change of pitch (usually higher) on a syllable within a word (accentuation) aids meaning and pronunciation.

  This is important for speakers whose first language isn't English. As a general rule nouns have their stress on the first syllable, verbs on the second.

  For example present present

  record record

  attribute attribute

  (where you put the main stress on part of a word changes the meaning)

- Change of pitch (usually higher) on words to emphasise their meaning.

For example 'This is the best of the three – roomed apartments' can be interpreted in four different ways corresponding to how you emphasise the key words.

Make sure you only emphasise key words, not subordinate ones such as in, on, for, as, is, the, of, etc...

This is the best of the three-roomed apartments

This is the best of the three-roomed apartments

This is the best of the three-roomed apartments

This is the best of the three-roomed apartments

Be careful also not to over-emphasise key words. Change of pitch is much more effective than using volume on key words.

Change to pitch (lower) on words to colour the meaning
For example 'She's in a grumpy mood today!' (it wouldn't be appropriate to raise the pitch on 'grumpy'.)
When we use antithesis (words emphasised by opposite ideas) the pitch changes from high to low.
e.g. 'I want this one, not that one.'

- Change in pitch upwards – to reflect a change of thought – at the beginning of a new idea / new paragraph.
- We lift our voice when listing points 1st/2nd/3rd
- A change a lower pitch when inserting a parenthesis. For example Joe Bloggs, (the leading actor) collapsed on stage.

Now let's think about how you sound normally? i.e. your usual pitch level. We each of us have our own natural pitch range. It's known as our 'optimum' pitch level. Make the sound "mmm" as if you're humming in agreement with something I've said. Say it again –

twice this time – they'll be a lower and higher "mmm" that's your 'optimum' pitch range. Lower generally for men and higher for women. I won't go into the technicalities here but be careful you don't push the voice above your natural pitch level (perhaps when projecting) or below your natural sounding voice (perhaps to sound gentle or sympathetic). It can be damaging to the vocal mechanism.

We can be tempted to push the voice over its natural range say when talking on a mobile phone and there's extra noise around you – in a shopping centre for instance, or a football match or a noisy swimming pool; you'll be aware of this as you can end up coughing and spluttering. As I mentioned earlier, with breathing – you're only aware of it when it feels uncomfortable, say after climbing a flight of stairs. And so it is with pushing your voice over its optimum pitch level – you feel the vocal strain and this can cause discomfort and possible damage to the vocal tract.

We can push our voices too when speaking over noise – in a bar, disco, a party. Also, if there is no microphone available – we can easily push the voice from the throat, as we strain to make ourselves heard. Audiences are known to chatter away if their speaker can't be heard.

Pace

Pace is the speed of our delivery – how fast or slow.

We need **variety / contrast** as a plodding regularity is soporific!

We need variation in the speed of delivery. How do we decide when to go faster or slower?

For example:

Faster – speaking with a sense of urgency, excitement, combined with higher pitch, also words in parenthesis.

Too fast – we can't take in words, appropriate speed to words – e.g. I'm so excited – say it slowly. (sounds sarcastic)

Slower – speaking with a seriousness in the voice – combined with lower pitch.

Slower on single words to bring out their meaning e.g. weary

Slower – end of speech, as you slow down, don't go quieter.

Slow down to highlight names, places, products, statistics, prices, phone numbers.

Pause

A pause is a cessation of speech – SILENCE – which can be as effective as speech.

Vary the length of pause otherwise we get plodding regularity.

- At phrases don't over pause.
- at the end of sentences. - longer/
- at commas – briefly
- at the end of paragraphs – end of an item - longer pause//

- if you're reading a poem, don't always pause at the end of a line. ↗ an enjambment or carry-on line, means that the line runs on and the word at the end of the line needs emphasising.
- pause – before and after "direct speech" and quotes between narrative and dialogue (remember your children's stories!)
- pause – before and after – names, figures, statistics.
- End of your talk– slow down and stop. SILENCE. Before you say 'Thank you' or start to sum up your main points.

Inflections

The up's and down's in the voice on the ends of words which express meaning to your listener. Inflection suggests the implications in our voice.

For example – when asking a question,

"Will you be going today?"

The voice rises at the end of the word. The voice falls at the end of the word in sentence beginning with question words. e.g. When does the post arrive?

A rising inflection generally indicates that the thought is incomplete and so connects one idea to the next. "We bought apples, oranges, bananas....

A falling inflection ↘ indicates that the thought is complete. A statement ends with a falling inflection.

e.g. We are going out, now say, We are going out? with a rising inflection on the last word of a sentence and you completely change the meaning from a statement, to a question.

A falling inflection ↘ is used in questions which begin with question – words (where, which, what, when, why).

It also implies finality and certainty. e.g. Will you be at the meeting tonight?

Reply – yes (doubtful)

Reply – yes (certain of the answer)

Inflections convey the implications in the voice than the actual words can convey.

We come back here to the primitive response that we have to the sounds within words, as we do with the other non-verbal signals. We listen to the intonations in the voice. The more expressive our voice can be, the easier it is for our listeners to understand our words, our message. As I've said earlier, don't make hard work for your audience; they will lose concentration and then you have lost them.

Volume

Variety of softness / loudness for effect and can be very effective too! A lower pitch, slower pace, a more serious tone and a quietness is very compelling. A higher pitch, an enthusiastic tone, a quicker pace and a louder delivery where appropriate can work very well. Use sparingly and keep separate from the overall volume level of your Speech.

To sum up then: Symbols to use to mark up your script; this notation acts as a guide so that you can relax and enjoy communicating with your audience.

Word Emphasis

We can emphasise words by

- a pause / or // before and after a word
- changing the pace /\/\/\/\ quicker

  .... slower

- change the pitch ↗ of the whole word, ↗ 'lift' the voice at the beginning of new ideas.
  or ↗ ↘ at the end of a word (inflection)
- ________ underline 'key' words
- ⌒ phrasing

Don't forget adjectives/adverbs 'colour' words! Don't gloss over them, as if they don't exist.

Where you want to sound enthusiastic, draw this symbol to remind you to sound that way!

Write out and use these symbols every single time you have something to say – actors do so, voiceovers do so, and Top-Notch Speakers definitely do so!

As an example, I'd like you to see how I'd **mark up a script** ready for delivery. However experienced you are it's something we all still do!

Good evening Ladies and Gentlemen /
My name is Gillian Cohen
and I'm your Chairman for this evening. //

I am delighted to welcome you all here
on this cold wintry evening /
to the first in a new series of workshops entitled
"Filling out your Tax Return" and all that... //

Our speaker is no stranger to our community,
having entertained us magnificently last winter
with his wit and expertise on his subject. //
May I introduce you once again to Mr Top-Notch Speaker.
....

In Conclusion

Preparing yourself, by adopting the right frame of mind and preparing your talk with your audience's needs at the forefront of your mind are the first steps towards becoming a Top-Notch speaker.

Becoming aware of the signals of our body language, how vital the right tone of voice is, obtained through the correct body alignment and centred breathing are the fundamentals of our subject. Professional Speakers know how important it is to connect with their audience, to project, to be clear and to be expressive. This is the creativeness of our work.

The following voice care tips are also very useful and surprisingly effective.

A dehydrated voice lacks resonance and expression. Your vocal mechanism can't work efficiently.

Speaking is very drying. Drink plenty of water. The caffeine in tea, coffee or cola act as a diuretic though.

- No Alcohol before or during your speech!
- You need to be firing on all cylinders! You don't need to dull your brain or slur your speech... until afterwards! Spirits are also very dehydrating.
- Smoking Dehydrates - compensate by drinking extra water.

- If you've got a cold, beware of remedies for drying your cold up – it will also dry up your vocal tract.
- A hot room, too many clothes – you will loss moisture through perspiration. Your vocal cords need moisture to work efficiently.
- A dry mouth signals nervousness, acts as a trigger to the brain, therefore before we know it, it's a downward spiral towards feeling totally out of control.
- Don't talk above noise at social events if you don't want to damage your voice. You'll end up hoarse and could lose your voice.
- Avoid repeated throat clearings – damaging to the voice and signals 'anxiety' to your audience.
- Tension either emotional or physical gives you the tell-tale lump in the throat, leading to a change in your breathing pattern and vocal strain.

Finally, I hope these 7 Steps have helped you feel more confident now about getting up on your feet and Speaking Out in Public. My aim – clear, expressive, natural speech, full of energy and vitality coupled with simple words spoken from the heart – gives you the ability to affect your audience with what you have to say. Once you have tasted success, felt well–deserved applause – it gives you such a sense of achievement, you'll come back for more I promise you!

Good luck and enjoy it all!
Gillian Cohen

Let me know how you get on. You can contact me via my publishers at www.mavenpublishingcompany.com

If you've found it interesting learning about the Spoken Word and would like to work further with a Voice Coach, please contact the following organisations, whose members are vetted re their qualifications and experience before they are put on their Professional Register.

Society of Teachers of Speech & Drama
www.stsd.org.uk

Voice Care Network
www.voicecare.org.uk

British Voice Association
www.british-voice-association.com